Rustic Furniture Makers

RUSTIC

Furniture Makers

Ralph Kylloe

SALT LAKE CITY

ABOUT THE COVER AND FRONT MATTER PHOTOGRAPHS

Cover photograph is a slab fantasy chair by Glen Burleigh of
Oregon. Octagonal & rectangular table-tops by Vito Decosmo. Table
and chairs on main title page by Hellers Fabulous Furniture.

This is a Peregrine Smith Book, published by
Gibbs Smith, Publisher
P.O. Box 667, Layton, Utah 84041

First Edition
98 97 96 95 6 5 4 3 2 1

Design by Leesha Jones
Edited by Gail Yngve
Printed in Singapore

Library of Congress Cataloging-in-Publication Data
Kylloe, Ralph R.
    Rustic furniture makers/Ralph Kylloe.
    p. cm.
    ISBN 0-87905-680-0
    1. Furniture making. 2. Country furniture.
3. Cabinetmakers.
I. Title.
TT194.K95 1995
749.213—dc20   95—11532
                                            CIP

And this our lives exempt from Public Haunt,

finds tongues in trees

books in running brooks,

sermons in stones and

good in everything.

—William Shakespeare (1564-1616)

from *As You Like It*

DEDICATION

Michele Keller first started working with me in 1992. We became inseparable

and have traveled continuously to antique shows, decorating projects, lectures,

and other events around the country. Along with being an exceptional artist,

she's also an excellent fisherman. I could do nothing less than marry her.

A man never had a better wife and friend.

CONTENTS

Rustic Furniture Makers

PREFACE

"A Good Place To Camp"
NORCROSS POND
BATHING ~ BOATING

VINE ST. FISHING CLUB

CAMP JOSEP

ABOVE: Yellow birch porch swing presently at a lodge in the Adirondacks, circa 1920.

OPPOSITE: Porch setting in 1930s New Hampshire. The huge birch chair was constructed in the Adirondacks, and the root hat tree is by Lee Fountain.

PREVIOUS PAGE: Stunning vanity made in Wyoming, circa 1900.

SINCE the publication of my book *Rustic Traditions* (Gibbs Smith, Publisher, 1993), I have been asked questions on many occasions about new rustic builders as well as the method of photography I used for the photos in that book.

In *Rustic Furniture Makers,* I sought to answer some of these questions as well as explore some of the different styles of rustic furniture that are being created around the country. I also wanted to introduce a few builders who have had little publicity but certainly deserve recognition for their efforts. I further sought to show several more examples of some of the classic antique pieces of vernacular rustic furniture that have recently "been discovered." Rustic furniture, in reality, has received little attention

Pair of Adirondack yellow birch cube chairs with root table found in the Catskills.

from the art world and, often, less attention from its owners who occasionally have neglected to properly care for the pieces. Consequently, I have always felt a pressing need to record and document rustic furnishings before they fall to the ravages of nature and man and are recalled back to earth.

Also in this book, I wanted to discuss details of the photographic methods we use because numerous people have asked how we got such rich, warm tones in many of the photos presented in my first book and, hopefully, in this book as well.

Regarding the photography, almost all of the photographs in *Rustic Traditions* and in *Rustic Furniture Makers* were shot in 35mm with a Nikon system; the film was Kodachrome 25. We used old studio floodlights that were diffused so that they subtly bounced over the subject matter.

Kodachrome 25 is a very slow film, and exposures were usually between one and two minutes long with the aperture set at F16. Because of the significant reciprocity failure of this film, we found that correct exposures were usually four times longer than the reading on a light meter.

There is quite a bit of guesswork in this system, but with a little bit of practice (as well as significant time alterations for exposures), it is a system that works well for us. We have always been a bit opposed to electronic strobes (although it is infinitely an easier method to light subject matter) since the light always seems flat and too even for our taste.

Rustic Furniture Makers focuses on documenting historic pieces of rustic furniture and also presents numerous new pieces of hand-made, one-of-a-kind, rustic furnishings. Though a large number of exceptionally well-made commercial pieces of rustic furniture exist today, coming specifically from the Old Hickory Furniture Company located today in Shelbyville, Indiana, the focus of this book is on one-of-a-kind pieces. However, for those wishing to peruse the past of Indiana hickory furnishings, my recently published book, *A History of the Old Hickory Furniture Company and the Indiana Hickory Furniture Movement*, is an ideal place to start.

My wife, Michele, and I traveled a great deal for this book, as well as for *Rustic Traditions*. We spent time with builders in California, Oregon, Wyoming, New York, New Hampshire, Michigan, and other areas as well as visiting many other states to see antique pieces along with new pieces that are currently residing in their new homes.

LEFT: Horn chair with hoof feet, produced anywhere from 1830 to 1930. The European lamp table and desk lamp of fallow deer is circa the 1890s.

LEFT: Table by Ernest Stowe of the Adirondacks. Stowe, who worked around the turn of the century, is recognized as America's greatest rustic furniture builder.

I want to thank all those who graciously accommodated Michele and me—for the use of spare bedrooms, the meals offered, and the charming hospitality. Special thanks goes out to my publisher Gibbs Smith and editors Madge Baird and Gail Yngve for their support with my projects that are important to me. Special thanks also to Clifton Montieth, Phil Clausen, Matt Madsen, Bill and Wendy Nolan, Brent McGregor, Lionel Maurier, Paul Fiori, Robert and Gayle Greenhill, Sarah Wildasin, John and Angela Kayman, Barbara and Thad Collum, Barry Gregson, Paul Allen, Ron Shanor, Glenn Burleigh, Ken Heitz, Jerry and Jessica Farrell, George Jacques, Gilbert Jacques, Elaine Rush, David Sellers, and numerous others whom I have forgotten to mention.

INTRODUCTION

RUSTIC furniture builders live the lives of artists and follow callings that few others hear. They maintain no specific educational pattern and are largely self-taught. In general, they come to the craft with highly developed skills and talents in areas such as music, computers, business, outdoor pursuits, as well as many others. They share, however, a passion for nature.

Initially, many of them were involved in traditional careers but withdrew from the mainstream because it was not "right for them." They are, in their own right, artists and entrepreneurs who have found the correct outlet for their creative passions.

Certainly not all individuals who build a twig stand or a chair create museum-quality pieces; however, the personal rewards for their creativity are self-evident. Still, a few builders have raised their particular efforts to the level of the artistic, and are particularly fortunate to be able to make a living as artists and craftspeople.

Today, there are several hundred individuals around the country who build rustic furniture. It is obvious that they cannot all be featured in this book. However, I have featured several individuals whose work is exceptional and deserving of recognition. It is unfortunate that more makers could not be acknowledged, but space limitations prevent their inclusion. Nevertheless, two great places to see many rustic builders all at once are the Western Design Conference held annually in Cody, Wyoming, and the Rustic Furniture Builders Show held at the Adirondack Museum in Blue Mountain Lake, New York.

ABOVE: Close-up view of the intricate work of Reverend Ben Davis.

BELOW: Very unusual tete-a-tete found in a brownstone mansion in Chicago. Constructed of elk antlers, the mid-Victorian piece has original purple upholstery.

For any rustic builder, the creation of a work of art out of natural materials elevates the human experience. The joy of creating rustic furniture is that there is so little manipulation of the natural materials. The building process is open to anyone who has an affinity for a few simple tools and a desire and a courage to create.

Traditionally, furniture building was the domain of men. Women, however, have now taken their rightful place in the rustic arts and often share in the creation of rustic crafts in cooperative ventures with men and on their own. Many couples find partaking in the art business both profitable and personally rewarding. It is interesting

ABOVE: Porch set by Reverend Davis. Each stick was hand-collected and intricately hand-carved with a pen knife.

ABOVE: A photograph of George Wilson, highly regarded Adirondack builder who constructed furniture in the early part of this century.

"SHRINE OF THE PINES" BALDWIN MICH. L-7

to note that although many men receive the accolades for their efforts, many of these same men freely admit that their wives are often the driving force behind their success. Frequently, it is the women who run the business as well as sand and finish products, make deliveries, load and unload trucks at ungodly hours, and lend an artistic eye to the creative process. Women's efforts within the industry are not unnoticed.

ABOVE: Sideboard and chairs by master builder Raymond W. Overholzer. The best-known furniture builder in Michigan, his entire collection of driftwood furniture is housed in Baldwin, Michigan.

LEFT: Studio portrait of man in rustic chair, circa 1980s.

ABOVE: Interior of Adirondack camp Top Ridge, the summer retreat of Mrs. Merriweather-Post, circa the 1920s.

Builders today either incorporate one or more different styles or create their own. Indigenous materials usually depict the type of furniture or artwork to be developed. Consequently, regional stylistic differences do exist. Among them are western rustic, twig, and Adirondack that includes mosaic and applied bark. Further styles include free-form rustic, which may include burls and stump-based items, and a final category that includes antler or horn pieces.

Builders are certainly not limited to these categories; many pieces incorporate different elements from each style. For instance, craftsman Brent McGregor creates chairs out of burled lodgepole pine and applied arms made of elk antlers. In short, builders are limited only by their imaginations and are somewhat restricted by the laws of comfort. Modern rustic builders, however, have effectively fused the requirements of function with the aesthetics of form to make one of the most profound art statements that exists within the creative processes of humans today.

ABOVE: Adirondacks, drop leaf table made in the 1920s. Chairs from the Rustic Hickory Furniture Company of LaPorte, Indiana.

RIGHT: Root plant stand in old black paint from the Victorian period is the home of an Indian souvenir tribe who stand guard over the immediate area.

ABOVE: Chair and table by Reverend Ben Davis.

RIGHT: Whimsy armchair constructed of cedar and rhododendron branches. The chair is strikingly full, freeform, and quite comfortable.

ABOVE: Victorian, bark-covered vanity with drawer and mirror. The antlers are from fallow deer.

LEFT: Display case from the Appalachian Mountain range. The piece, probably constructed around 1920, contains elements of whimsy and freedom often found in rustic furnishings.

ABOVE: Birch-bark desk made in the early part of this century by a builder in the Adirondacks.

RIGHT: Set of four dining chairs by Reverend Davis.

"SHRINE OF THE PINES" BALDWIN, MICH.   L·6

ABOVE: Pair of beds by Raymond W. Overholzer.

RIGHT: Tall desk built by Ernest Stowe of the Adirondacks. The intricate inlay and form are indicative of an individual who had a great appreciation and understanding of the art world.

Costs of antique rustic furniture have skyrocketed within the past few years. The majority of the advanced pieces being produced today are better conceived and executed than pieces of the past. In fact, many of the really great contemporary pieces are underpriced when compared to other endeavors within the art market as a whole. Because of the recent interest and surge in the prices of antique rustic furnishings (as well as the almost total unavailability of them), it only stands to reason that many new items on the market are considerably undervalued. Now may be the perfect time to invest in art produced by today's high-end rustic artists.

The process of building rustic furniture is not complicated. Building comfortable, aesthetically pleasing furniture is, and often, accomplished builders have spent many years perfecting their art.

Wood is collected during the winter months, when the bark will adhere to the trees, and dried for months to ensure its durability and prevent further shrinkage. Summer is an ideal time to harvest bark because the sap is down, and it can be easily peeled from trees.

A number of builders use the most simple tools available, and some builders, such as Jack Leadley of the Adirondacks, use no power tools whatever. Other builders, such as Lionel Maurier of New Hampshire, construct complicated projects and require the use of sophisticated woodworking equipment. Construction techniques differ from builder to builder, but little has changed in the basic construction of simple rustic furniture in the past hundred years.

ABOVE: Washstand made of twigs probably around the 1920s. The piece was originally from West Virginia.

ABOVE: Hand-carved decorative floor lamp with skin, handpainted shade, circa the 1920s.

LEFT: Tall armchair with original cotton upholstery. The chair was found in Maine and is on original casters.

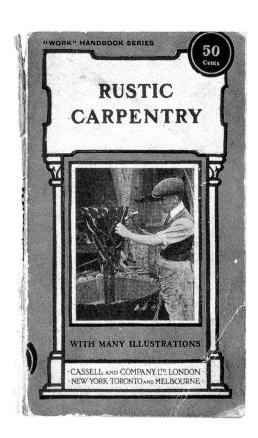

LEFT: Small paperback book published in 1907 includes plans for numerous pieces of rustic furniture and lessons on how to construct them.

BELOW: Small root-based table probably from Lee Fountain of the Adirondacks. A mosaic star pattern is inlaid in the top of the table.

RIGHT: Black Forest Victorian antler mirror over a 1930s sycamore desk. Mica Lamp by Michael Adams of Aurora Studios.

Branches, logs, roots, and twigs are fitted together in a variety of ways to produce functional and artistic forms that make up today's rustic furniture. Some builders use hammers and nails, and one maker simply uses rope to tie sticks together to create chairs and settees. Most advanced builders, however, mortise and tenon the joints on their work to ensure sturdiness and longevity.

Oftentimes, individuals incorporate antlers, pine cones, or other natural objects to add embellishments and individuality to their products. Further still, some builders, including Jessica Farrell and Barney Bellinger, add paintings to their works for originality. Usually, these paintings are of natural scenes that include moose, bear, lakes and mountain scenes.

ABOVE: Stump-based yellow birch bark table found on a front porch in the Lake George region of the Adirondacks. The elk antlers and the desk set are turn-of-the-century and the lamp is contemporary.

ABOVE: A den in a rustic New Hampshire log cabin. The lounge is made by Indiana Willow Products.

Pieces are then finished with either polyurethane, varnish, tung oil, or other sealing products to protect the wood and other materials. In general, the construction of rustic furniture has changed little in the past hundred years. Designs have certainly changed that reflect the individuality and creativity of their makers. But the construction of rustic furniture is open to all who seek a creative outlet with natural materials.

ABOVE: Small Adirondack birch desk. The wall clock is by Ernest Stowe.

RUSTIC furnishings had its beginnings with the dawn of the human race. No doubt some individual, after struggling throughout the day, rolled a fallen log in front of a fire to watch the "catch of the day" cook. The fallen log certainly sufficed for eons as the principal piece of furniture for those who first sought a place to sit.

I imagine that this initial piece of furniture was quite pleasant. Logs were plentiful, and if they were at all un-comfortable, one could simply throw them on the fire, which in turn kept the insects and beasts away. The fires also provided light, a place for comradeship, and warmth on cold winter nights.

ABOVE: Advertisement photograph of a rustic gate in Thomasville, Georgia.

PREVIOUS PAGE: This 1910 drop-front desk was constructed of branches from lodge-pole pines in the northern Rocky Mountain area. It was found at a Wyoming ranch.

I suspect that with time and the advent of crude tools, our relatives were able to hack away any uncomfortable knobs or branches on the fallen logs to make them just a bit more pleasant for sitting. As we progressed further, our ancestors discovered that by adding a few leaves, pine boughs, and later, cushions, the chairs became more comfortable and other items of furniture gradually came into existence until tables, bookcases, and Lazy-boy recliners began filling many of the households around the world.

RIGHT: Handmade twig chair from Maine.

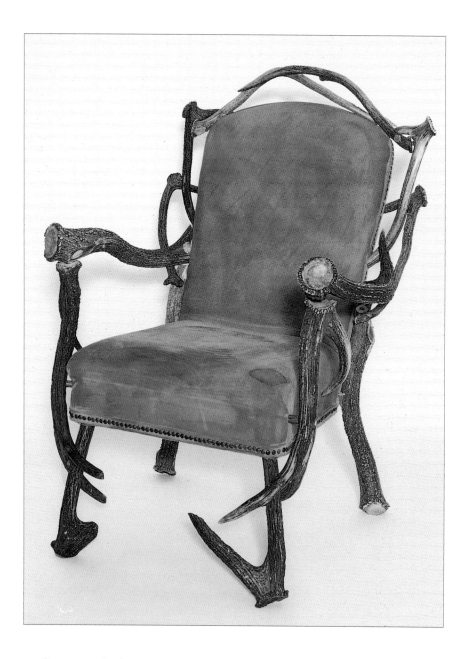

Some people, however, were stubborn. They refused to fall prey to the advent of technology, or out of necessity, simply continued to make furniture that incorporated the elements of nature within their designs. Rather than disguise or alter materials in such a way that the user would find it difficult to identify the actual material that was used in the piece, they incorporated the folly of nature into their artifacts. It is so often intriguing (and discouraging) to hear craftspeople describe how they were inspired by nature to create a piece of art, and then completely alter the natural materials used within the piece as if to hide, disguise, or deny that the materials had anything to do at all with nature.

Folk art is classically defined as "art created by untrained or un-skilled craftspeople." I suspect that many of those past builders as well as a few of today's builders of rustic furnishings fall into that category. But why create furniture in the first place?

LEFT: Elk-antler armchair probably from the 1930s.

ABOVE: Raymond W. Overholzer's massive dining room set.

RIGHT: Studio portrait from the late 1880s. Photographers commonly used rustic furniture as studio props in the Victorian period and later.

ABOVE: Adirondack cube chairs and stump-based table with bird-cage gallery from the turn of the century.

ABOVE: Game room at the Eddy Lodge in Wisconsin. The pieces shown are constructed of massive cedar logs as is the rest of the furniture in the building.

ABOVE: Turn-of-the-century family portrait. The chairs are classical rockers that are often found in the Appalachian Mountains.

Educators today recognize a cognitive developmental process referred to as "the theory of maximum arousal." The theory suggests that individuals best exist and are most complete when they are enriched and stimulated, and all people have different stimulation levels.

Imagine, if you will, that certain automobiles are built to best run at certain speeds and not at others. This is how humans are. Some people are at their best when they are creating, and others are not; our brains are built that way. Consider the quilter who resides in the country free from needs and wants. She has what she needs but continues to quilt for the pure joy of it. She is most aroused, and most alive, when doing what she does best. A need for peace within ourselves compels us to look closely at our lifestyles and to incorporate values of importance into our routines. Humans have a profound need to create things with their own hands; the more personal the products we create, the more meaning they have for us as individuals. Our efforts create traditions, and these traditions ground us to the world.

LEFT: Interior of a resort and tavern in northern Wisconsin in the 1920s.

BELOW: Business card from a rustic furniture builder.

Rustic furniture can be defined as artifacts constructed of twigs, branches, bark, roots, tree trunks, antlers, or horns in such a way as not to disguise or alter the materials used within construction. The bark is often left on the wood, and the natural contortions, twists, and contours of the material are incorporated into the finished product. The material is not highly manipulated in the name of art, and no attempt is made to disguise the material. The builders sought to maintain the integrity of materials they were using. Items built in this way incorporate the natural beauty of nature.

ABOVE: Individuals on late Victorian cedar settee.

Rustic furniture is full of movement and often has the appearance that it is about to get up and dance. The pieces maintain movement, and the forms appear to be in motion. Often, we have a tendency to view the organic as grotesque, almost like steam rising from warm water or tens of thousands of ants scurrying in a small area. These phenomena have motion, and humans feel a certain drawing or closeness with that organic quality. We find this easier to comprehend if we imagine watching a fire, fast-moving clouds, or ocean waves. It is that freedom that calls us and for which words are not adequate. We just know that

it is a part of us, and we revel in the mystery and magical elements inherent in nature.

Other pieces within the genre of rustic furniture are items that have been inlaid with tiny twigs and often referred to as mosaic. Some forms of art within the world today are often referred to as compulsive or obsessive. This description certainly can be attributed to mosaic forms of rustic furniture as often hundreds and even thousands of small twigs are meticulously cut and placed on the surface of a rustic piece in a variety of interesting patterns as decoration.

ABOVE: Mid-Victorian portrait of a family posing on an outdoor rustic settee.

ABOVE: Yellow birch-bark table made by Earl Rector in the late 1920s.

LEFT: Mid-Victorian tin-type studio portrait.

ABOVE: Intricate gazebo probably from the lower New York area. Few of these outdoor pieces remain because of the continued exposure to the elements.

LEFT: This massive bark cupboard recently emerged at a Paris flea market and is presently in Colorado.

BELOW: Outdoor studio late Victorian tin-type.

One structure, easily the size of a small gymnasium, was recently discovered in the Vermont mountains. It was the receptacle of efforts made by the obsessive individuals who resided there in the 1930s. The room was completely lined with hundreds of thousands of twigs arranged in intricate patterns on the walls, doors, and ceiling of the building. Apparently, the project took the individual over ten years to complete, and, unfortunately, he died in a fire before completing the outside of the building.

What kind of a person would spend ten years decorating a hall with tiny twigs? The question is best left to the psychiatrists of the world, but certainly obsessive-compulsive can be used to describe the individual artist as well as his art.

There is a bit of danger, however, when we use clinical words to describe individuals. People who are meticulous and oriented to detail are certainly not always obsessive-compulsive, but I must admit that I often wonder about an individual who would utilize hundreds of thousands of fragments, albeit, twigs, matchsticks, shards, or other items to create or adorn pieces that we call art.

A sweet day dream

in PHILADELPHIA, PA.

LEFT: Romantic postcards from the late Victorian period commonly showed young couples relaxing on rustic furniture.

BELOW: Elk-antler chandelier constructed by Paul Allen of Fort Collins, Colorado.

In reality, many of the early rustic builders around the country were simple individuals who worked with simple tools and simple materials. They often lacked the articulation necessary to espouse the virtues and values of their attempts at art. Still, necessity being the mother of invention, many of these builders constructed wonderful things that, fortunately, we are beginning to understand and appreciate today.

As we enter the twenty-first century, society has reestablished the "back to nature" movement and a new appreciation for "things natural" has become apparent. Today, many individuals are cognizant of their roots to the earth and seek to become part of nature and not apart from it.

Consequently, all manner of folk art is being created today as people become aware of the intrinsic joys inherent in the art world and the act of creation. Empirical evidence can be found on a Sunday-afternoon drive down a country road—the whirligigs, picnic benches, painted animals, dolls, quilts, or numerous other folk-art attractions made by industrious folk artists and related cottage industries. Creativity is the passion that drives us along the road of enhancement, actualization, and enlightenment.

ABOVE: Stunning Gothic root chair in old, multi-colored paint. Often surfacing in the South, several of these chairs have surfaced recently in Maine where they are thought to be constructed by the Penobscot Indians for souvenir trade.

ABOVE: This enormous contemporary rhododendron settee is by Jerry Farrell.

LEFT: A stunning 1910 armchair built by Adirondack builder Ray Fininnin in the Upper St. Regis Lake region.

ABOVE: Armchair and table by Dave Robinson, recently displayed at the Adirondack Museum, Blue Mountain, New York.

Along with the more classical endeavors into the country folk-art genre, rustic furniture is once again being created by furniture makers, and it is receiving wide recognition for its innovativeness, style, and design.

In the past, rustic-furniture styles were often dictated by the materials indigenous to the regions where the craftspeople resided. By examining the regional differences, I find that Florida builders often used cypress trees; builders in the Appalachians used rhododendron branches; Adirondack craftspeople had available to them birch bark, cedar, and a variety of hardwoods; and western builders often used lodgepole pines and antlers in their products.

The Industrial Revolution not only gave us the technology to create things unheard and unthought of in the prior century, but it also gave us the need to escape the pressures and travails of daily lives in the factories and sweatshops. Conversely, people sought refuge in the peace and comfort of the wilderness regions of the country.

Folk artistry sprang up in all these areas, and individuals found that they could make a living out of creating wonderful rustic furniture of all shapes and sizes for the porches of resorts, cabins, retreats, and camps. Not only was this possible, but they also realized that they could create souvenirs for the folks back home as a reminder of the passions and peace of rustic settings. Consequently, folk artists made all sorts of rustic souvenirs, including birch-bark picture frames, miniature canoes, tepees, and canoe paddles, as well as all sorts of hand-carved animals and paintings.

RIGHT: Contemporary desk by Glenn Bauer; chair by John and Shirl Stacy. Both pieces were recently exhibited at the Rustic Furniture Builders show in the Adirondacks.

ABOVE: Stunning, tall, case clock by Clifton Montieth of Michigan. Montieth is known internationally for his unique designs and innovations.

For those individuals who could not venture into the wilds, some city planners created parks full of rustic accents including settees and chairs, gazebos, pergolas, and other adornments that allowed the user to experience the recuperative value of nature and natural things without having to leave the city.

In the past ten years, the movement has received considerable attention, and new rustic-furniture builders have brought the art to new heights. Builders all around the country are creating new styles and interpretations of passionate themes inherent in nature, and the public is actively supporting their efforts.

Admittedly, much of the new furniture being created today shows an influence from generations past. A few individuals, however, are creating designs and styles so innovative that their efforts have been widely noticed. For instance, Clifton Monteith of Michigan has created a style uniquely his own using the shoots of willow trees. Matt Madsen of California creates unique clocks and telephones. Phil Clausen of Oregon creates unusual lamps out of single pieces of wood.

RIGHT: One of a pair of contemporary settees by Clifton Monteith of Michigan.

BELOW: Dining room set by contemporary rustic builder Brent McGregor of Oregon. McGregor is known for fashioning innovative, comfortable furniture in the style of the old West.

Brent McGregor, also of Oregon, uses juniper trees for making beds, tables, and other furniture. Barry Gregson of the Adirondacks makes a variety of furniture out of materials found in his area, and Jerry Farrell and his wife, Jessica, also of New York, create innovative clocks and other furniture with intricate mosaic patterns inlaid on the surface of the pieces.

Numerous other craftspeople around the country are creating significant pieces of functional artwork that now grace the homes of thousands of individuals who have taken to collecting and utilizing rustic furniture for their home and porches.

ABOVE: Redwood furniture by Matt Madsen of California, best known for his custom clocks and telephones, sold worldwide.

The Artists Within Us

NO ONE GROUP OF PEOPLE can be described as unique from others. Although we have our differences, we are all humans and on the same journey. Individuality and uniqueness, however, abounds throughout the human race, and heroism exists at all levels of humanity. We would probably not be alive today if each of us did not possess a certain heroic quality, a profound motivation to survive, and a sense of our own uniqueness. Life, for most, would not be worth living if we did not or could not revel in our own individuality.

ABOVE: Small root table by Sampson Bog.

OPPOSITE: Studio portrait probably made in the 1880s.

PREVIOUS PAGE: A variety of rustic decorative items in a New Hampshire home.

Art is a gift from the heavens. It is available to all of us and has the capacity to permeate every endeavor and moment of our lives. Without art, most lives would be meaningless and filled with ennui. Although the artistic experience is within the grasp of us all, many fail to strive for the experience or recognize its inherent ability to increase the quality of our lives. The lesson of art to younger generations should be the prime responsibility of each generation. The structure, discipline, responsibility, beauty, joy, and passion within the artistic experience elevates living creatures and provides a sense of joy and goodness that brings meaning to our lives and advances our species as a whole. It has been said that without art, life is not worth living.

Modern philosophers and psychologists often refer to the phenomena of flow or peak experiences. During this time, people are said to be in contact with themselves and fully integrated; they lose a sense of time; they are at peace with themselves; they are fully functioning, spontaneous, in control, decisive, and equally important; they have a heightened sense of creativity and ability to concentrate.

The sensations mentioned above are often experienced by different individuals once they become involved in various endeavors. These endeavors are certainly not restricted to artists in the traditional sense. Anyone involved in almost any experience can achieve the above if her heart is in the activity. I have so often derived great pleasure watching sushi chefs, bakers, dishwashers, seamstresses, typists, musicians, runners, and numerous other individuals who have elevated their particular activities to an art form. Their lives are enhanced, and the world is a better place because of it.

BELOW: Exceptionally long hall table by Barry Gregson of Schroon Lake, New York.

RIGHT: Extraordinary tall floor lamp by Phil Clausen. The wood for this lamp is over five hundred years old. The lamp itself weighs over five hundred pounds.

ABOVE: Settee by Ken Heitz of the Adirondacks.

Nevertheless, there is a dark side to the human experience as well. In each of us is the capacity for rage, anger, and violence. Hence, our fascination with murder trials, death, wars, violent films, and despair. Occasionally, rustic furniture speaks to the dark side of the human condition as well. Often the twists, gnarls, and contortions expose our own fascination with the evil within each of us. Its grotesqueness often speaks to a part of us that most of us prefer to deny and/or relegate to the far regions of our minds. It frightens us and leaves us vulnerable to our own weaknesses. Nature knows no forgiveness or pity, and it is exactly that, and our own potential for aggressiveness, which can frighten and humble humans.

ABOVE: Interior of a Wisconsin lodge in the 1920s. It was common to find such lodges decorated with rustic furniture, Indian artifacts, and taxidermy.

LEFT: Sycamore frame constructed of dozens of bark pieces meticulously assembled by Nick Nickerson of the Adirondacks.

LEFT: Cupboard by
George Jacques of
Keene, New York. He
is the third
generation in his
family to build rustic
furniture.

In the art world, it is safe to explore our passions. Society usually tolerates expressions through art and certainly frowns on the infliction of our angers on others. Art allows us to relieve our stresses and anxieties through musical instruments, paint brushes, tools of all kinds, exercise, writing, dance and a plethora of sports activities. Art is safe and ameliorates our passions into a socially acceptable and desirable entity that can advance the hopes and causes of the human race. Involvement in art lessens our fears and civilizes our angers.

Nonetheless, many forms of art speak deeply to our primal instincts. Many of us experience a celebration or enhancement of our senses as we view certain pieces of rustic furniture. Many pieces touch us deeply as we sense their twists and contortions.

At the same time, we are occasionally repulsed by the rawness of nature inherent in the natural materials utilized by rustic-furniture builders. I have often heard reactions of "I hate this stuff" or "It's so grotesque" to certain styles of rustic furniture. In response, I have often wondered what are the real feelings that this viewer is experiencing? Does it remind him so much of his own primal passions? Are her own personal dragons coming forth to haunt her? Does it reveal things within us that we both fear and loathe? Does it stir some ancient emotions that we have long tried to deny?

I am convinced the answer to the above questions is yes. It certainly does stir up passions that we despise. However, it is a good thing to be reminded occasionally that we are, in reality, products of nature, and no matter how far we remove ourselves from our origins, it is our very nature that reminds us of whom and what we really are.

ABOVE: Postcard from the late Victorian period.

ABOVE: Studio portrait from the late 1880s. Photographers commonly used rustic furniture as studio props in the Victorian period and later.

ABOVE: Couch set built by Ron Shanor of Cody, Wyoming.

RIGHT: Children posing on an interesting rustic-style bench.

Phil Clausen

PREVIOUS PAGE: The organic works of Phil Clausen are unique in the rustic furniture field.

RIGHT: Phil Clausen relaxing in an extraordinary chair made from the base of a redwood tree.

PHIL CLAUSEN is an original. His works are so unusual that they stand alone in the realm of art within the tradition of rustic furniture. I first met Phil at his house in Oregon where he works with his son and other family members. He is a quiet and unassuming man who has the capacity to immediately put visitors at ease. His furniture, inspired solely by nature, is extraordinary.

Now in his mid-sixties, he started out as a third-generation dairy farmer. As a youth, he took great pleasure in building tree houses and enjoying the Coquille Valley where he still resides. He started building rustic furniture in the mid-seventies because selling real estate was "not fun." He was profoundly inspired by nature, mushrooms in particular, which often serve as the model for his furniture.

Clausen's most enticing accomplishments are his lamps. His floor lamps maintain an awesome presence and are often the centerpieces of the rooms where they are placed. Weighing up to seven hundred pounds each, they offer a very subtle, rich, and warm glow when lit. Like his table lamps and sconces, his lamps seem to grow directly from the surface they are resting on and appear to be organically connected to the room in which they reside.

Clausen uses a wide variety of woods and acquires materials from loggers in the region where he lives. Because of the great weight of the wood he uses for many of his projects, he often has to have materials delivered to his workshop with cranes and flatbed trucks.

At lunch on the day of my visit, about fifteen of us sat around a massive redwood table constructed by Phil. During the course of the meal, he commented that the slab for the tabletop was a little over a thousand years old. His reverence and admiration for his building materials were evident in his speech.

Phil, like almost all other rustic builders, is a self-taught craftsman whose enhancements turn a piece of deadwood into an object of profound beauty. He sells his objects worldwide, and the often-several-month wait for his artwork is well worth the time.

LEFT: The mantle for this fireplace was constructed by Clausen from a single piece of wood several hundred years old.

Diane Cole

I FIRST met Diane Cole at the Western Design Conference held annually in Cody, Wyoming. She was one of many rustic furniture builders who were exhibiting their works to an admiring public. At the conclusion of the conference, a dinner party and dance was held for the participants. To get some fresh air, I ventured out into the late evening and watched the sunset over the Rocky Mountains. Outside were a few individuals who greeted me with the usual warmth of the friendly people who reside in the West. Diane Cole was one of those people. As we admired the sunset, Diane handed me a bottle of tequila and informed me that we were now going to "Howl at the Moon."

After a few minutes, Diane started "howling" at the top of her lungs in a rather high-pitched voice. Much to my astonishment, her friends also began howling, too, and not wanting to feel left out, I joined in. Initially, I felt quite foolish and wondered just what we were trying to do, but after several moments, the coyotes in the background returned our calls. We all took great satisfaction in the response to our efforts. Diane later confided in me that howling "let's me feel wild." No doubt it does!

Diane is one of a growing number of women who build rustic furniture. She has a degree in range science but started building rustic furniture in 1979 after seeing a rustic chair in a magazine. In general, she does not build small pieces; rather, she prefers to construct large-scale items. Her appreciation of symmetry and form is evident in her work. Diane, like almost all other builders, is completely self-taught and, initially, she had to get over her fear of chain saws and power tools.

As a toddler, she climbed trees before she could walk, and she is the only woman, legend goes, that has climbed to the top of a particular sixty-foot mango tree in Honduras. When asked about the fact that she is one of only a few women rustic builders, she comments that she is surprised that so many men actually build rustic furniture. "With their curves and roundness, trees are completely feminine," she says. "Trees

BELOW: Cupboard by Diane Cole.

are so graceful. They reach toward the unknown."

Diane runs a one-woman shop and sells her projects privately and in galleries throughout the West. Her son, Jason Lohbeck, who worked with her for many years, now runs his own rustic furniture shop in Butte, Montana.

Gilbert Jacques

ABOVE: Probably the most accomplished of the modern Adirondack builders, Gilbert Jacques's furniture is elegant, graceful, and highly sought after.

PREVIOUS PAGE: The home of Gib Jacques is complete with furniture constructed with his own hands.

"GIB" JACQUES, a lifelong resident of the Adirondacks, took up building rustic furniture at age fifty when doctors suggested he find a hobby as physical therapy for a recent stroke. Now, nearly thirty years later, Gib is recognized as one of the great modern builders of rustic furniture in the Adirondacks. He is a man with a great smile, a passion for his work, and certainly not someone to be "messed with."

When I first met him, I jokingly asked where he bought all the rustic furniture that graced his home. His first reaction, with a little smile, was to say that he had "beaten up people for less than that." His lightheartedness and constant bantering with his wife and other visitors immediately put me at ease as he gave me the tour of his home and workshop.

During the visit, he mentioned that some months prior, a woman had ordered a table from him, and, even though he had asked to be paid for it upon delivery, she still had not paid him a month after having received the table.

"Well, she called me one morning and asked me if I could repair a small crack in the tabletop, and I told her to bring the table over. As soon as the table was back in my driveway, I took out the chain saw and sawed it in half," he recalled.

Once the horrified couple saw what Gib had done, the husband told his wife that this guy was crazy, and they jumped in their car and left. After that incident, no one ever "borrowed" anything from him again.

Gib is a man who does what is necessary to survive. The local dentist ordered several pieces of furniture from him, and Gib traded his furniture to him for a new set of false teeth. "Best deal I ever made," he said.

Gib's furniture is exquisite. He works in a classical Adirondack style, and the bureaus and other case pieces made by him are well proportioned and well constructed.

His beautifully detailed tables and chairs are functional. The designs applied to the surfaces of his pieces are stylistically original.

Since he often uses hardwoods or other exotic woods for the tops of different pieces, many of his earlier items have aged to a rich golden brown. He also made many miniature rustic chairs that, today, along with his full-size pieces, are eagerly sought after and prized by their owners.

Because of poor health problems, Gib has recently retired from rustic-furniture building. However, his nephew George Jacques, who is a retired state policeman, often worked with Gib on different rustic furniture projects and is now producing professionally crafted and artistic pieces in the Adirondack style as well.

RIGHT: Root-based table and miniature furniture by Gib Jacques. He is one of only a few builders who utilized exotic hardwoods for the tops of his pieces. Today his early pieces have mellowed to a rich warm patina.

ABOVE: Desk, lamp, chair, and library table by Gib Jacques. Gibs's use of linear forms greatly enhances the organic qualities of free-form wood.

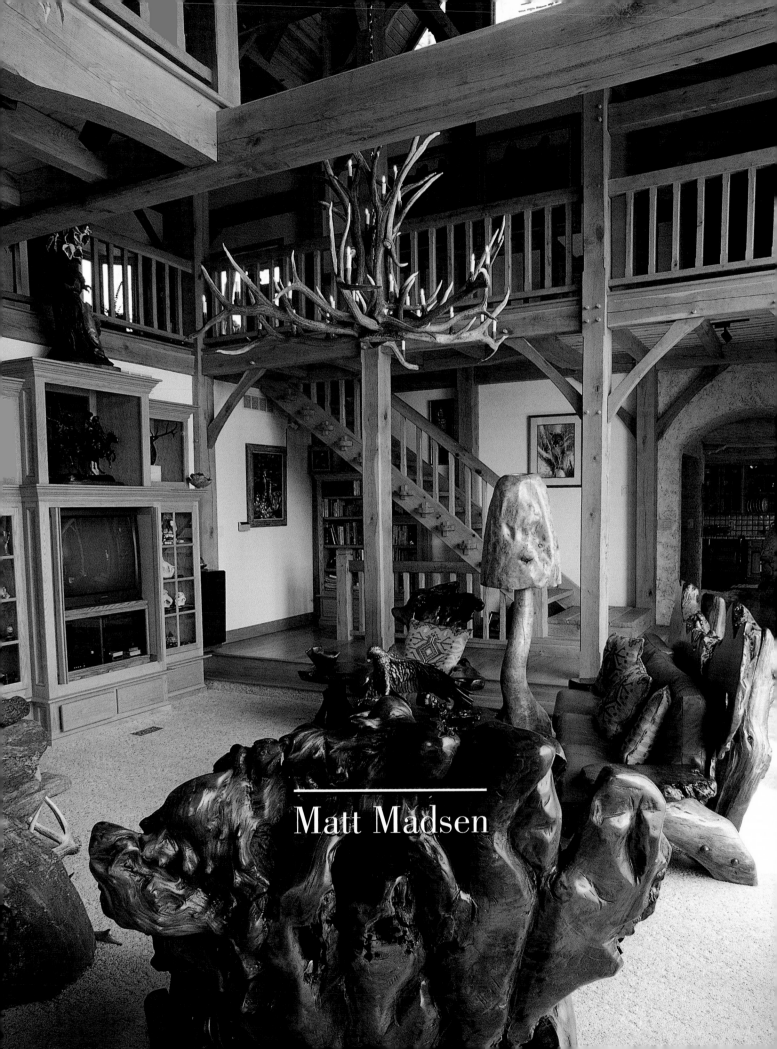

Matt Madsen

Matt often works with redwood from the huge stands near his home and gallery. He, like other builders, often uses pieces rejected by logging companies, and his front yard is littered with huge stumps and branches that eventually become his clocks, tables, and lamps. Matt's protege and business partner, Tim Duncan, works with him and produces unique items of his own, including breakfast sets and rocking chairs.

PREVIOUS PAGE: Redwood-slab set by Matt Madsen is the focal point of the room.

LEFT: Matt Madsen relaxing in his yard, a storage site for hundreds of tree roots that eventually will become furniture.

BELOW: Rocking chair by Madsen protege and business partner Tim Duncan.

RIGHT: Tall clock by Matt Madsen. His works are sold to customers around the world.

NEXT PAGE: Redwood-slab set by Madsen.

FIFTY-NINE-YEAR-OLD Matt Madsen has been building rustic furniture since 1981. He is certainly one of the best-known builders, and his furniture has been sold from his gallery in Orick, California, to customers in over thirty different countries. His first exposure to rustic furniture was as the owner of a lodge in Wyoming. A salesman showed him a few pieces built by a local craftsman, and Matt was immediately inspired. Within a short time, he made the decision to return to California, where he taught himself the craft of rustic furniture building.

Although he is often inspired by the works of others, he does not copy their works. Many of his most original creations were inspired by dreams in the middle of the night. He realizes, however, that nature does most of the work and that he, as a craftsman, turns nature into functional objects.

Brent McGregor

ABOVE: Juniper floor lamp by Brent McGregor.

PREVIOUS PAGE: Bedroom furniture by Brent McGregor. Sleeping in this bed gives one the distinct feeling of sleeping under the trees. Brent is one of only a few individuals who uses juniper trees for a wide variety of projects.

LEFT: Brent McGregor at home in the woods.

BRENT MCGREGOR is an adventurer at heart. As a youth, he traveled to Canada where he paddled a canoe to Alaska, and was on the ocean for thirty days by himself. He lived in an Alaskan tepee with eighteen sled dogs for more than a year, the temperatures often reaching fifty degrees below zero. During that time, he made all his own clothing from the hides and skins of animals that he trapped.

For a time, he worked as a logger and in 1980 started building log homes. In 1986, he began to also build rustic furniture.

Brent describes his efforts in metaphysical terms. Often while walking in the woods near his home in Oregon and looking for materials, he enters a realm that can only be described as spiritual. Seeing the shapes and formations in the trees is a meditative experience for him, and the designs for his furniture come from within himself. He defines his furniture as an extension of himself, and his products as a

reflection of his own personality. He lives close to nature with a house and huge yard full of extraordinary materials and furniture as well as a friendly group of chickens, goats, and cats. It is an exceptional place to visit as the desert surroundings are enhanced by a mountain background and coyotes howling in the night.

Brent has, like many other passionate artists, a disarming personality, and one immediately feels at ease around him. His quiet

ABOVE: Probably the most extraordinary rustic bed ever created, constructed by Brent McGregor of contorted juniper trees.

confidence and passionate interests in what others are doing is part of his charm. He is admirable because of his unpretentiousness and sincerity.

Brent's furniture is unique and tempered with great feeling. He has managed to create a style all his own. The designs of many of his pieces are incredibly original, and he often incorporates a variety of woods and antlers into single items. The pieces are consistently comfortable and structurally sound. He refuses to mass-produce his pieces, and he still delights in the handcrafted aspects of his endeavors. His pieces are eagerly sought after by his clients with whom he enjoys considerable personal contact. They do not mind the often-long wait for his remarkable artwork.

Jerry and Jessica Farrell

JERRY FARRELL is one of many unique characters in the rustic-furniture business. He has been building rustic furniture since 1972, and his efforts are now almost legendary. A number of the best collections around the country maintain a piece or two of his products.

Jerry approaches art with an overt passion and intensity that is evident in both his work and personality. He is a man of many opinions, and converses quite comfortably about a variety of subjects. In recent years, his wife, Jessica, has joined in the business, and she handpaints the scenes that embellish the many clocks, frames, and case pieces produced by Jerry.

In the late 1960s, after the Kent State incident, Jerry left college and hitchhiked north to Alaska. There, he supported himself by playing honky-tonk piano in several Yukon taverns. After his Alaskan stay, he worked with a traveling circus, playing an antique pump organ for the puppet sideshow.

ABOVE: Detail work of a clock by Jerry Farrell.

Having always worked with wood, Jerry began one day to build furniture out of local stands of yellow birch trees. "The materials were free, and I needed very few tools to get started," he comments.

The mosaic work on Jerry's pieces is superb. His craftsmanship is exceptional, and his designs are often quite original.

Jessica's paintings are well executed and rich in natural colors. The scenes usually include moose, bear, and natural settings.

The Farrells sell their artwork around the country through a number of galleries and to private customers. They also exhibit at the Rustic Furniture Builders show that is held in the fall of each year at the Adirondack Museum in upstate New York.

LEFT: Mantle clock by Jerry and Jessica Farrell.

BELOW: An assortment of exquisitely crafted pieces by Jerry and Jessica Farrell of New York, recently exhibited at the Adirondack Museum, Blue Mountain, New York.

Ron Shanor

Ron's work is well conceived and well proportioned, and his chairs are quite comfortable. His simplistic approach to his craft is evident in that the pieces are not heavily adorned or too complex. His choice of natural materials are statements by themselves, and the burls and natural contortions in the wood are well integrated into his pieces.

Ron sells his wares from six different galleries in the Colorado, Wyoming, and Montana area, as well as privately. His wife shares in the family business and frequently works on the pieces with Ron.

RON SHANOR is described by some craftsmen as the "new kid on the block," having just come to the rustic-crafting business in 1990. As a boy, he worked in his father's workshop and later became a machinist. From there, he and his wife, Jean, started a greenhouse and landscaping business. About four years ago, Ron decided to try his hand at building rustic furniture. Surprisingly, he has been most influenced by Victorian furniture and style, although his own furniture does not show it. He does admit that he has no great or grandiose orientation to the art world and that his approach to his efforts has always been toward the simplistic.

PREVIOUS PAGE: Dining room set by Ron Shanor, who works in a classical western style.

ABOVE: Ron Shanor at his home.

RIGHT: Cupboard by Shanor of Cody, Wyoming.

FAR RIGHT: Desk set by Shanor.

Barry Gregson

WHEN ASKED to name their favorite builders, those who construct rustic furnishings often put the name of Barry Gregson at the top of their lists.

As a youth Barry was a productive individual. He made his own kites, boomerangs, and other toys. He was a firm believer in finding the materials for anything he needed in the woods. A self-taught individual, if he couldn't figure something out, he read books for further information. He, like so many other builders, is also an accomplished musician, having played guitar in numerous bands around the country.

Barry spent the first eighteen years of his working life as a stonemason. Many of the well-built homes and other structures in the Adirondacks have fireplaces and stone porches built by him.

Surprisingly, Barry's furniture has been most influenced by Early American furniture rather than contemporary or early rustic builders. The furniture made by Barry is not only well designed but surprisingly comfortable as well. Sets of his dining and armchairs made more than a decade ago are still structurally tight and have mellowed to a rich, golden patina.

The furniture by Barry Gregson has presence. It is not only significant in its own right, it is sophisticated art. Despite this presence, the organic quality of his furniture blends with the environment, and his pieces seem to fit naturally into the spaces that they occupy.

ABOVE: Barry Gregson at his home in the Adirondacks.

LEFT: Paddle armchair by Barry Gregson.

Barry's family is also involved in the rustic-furniture business. His wife, Darlene, runs his gallery. His two sons, Matthew and Dylan, work with him as builders. His eleven-year-old daughter, Skye, is an accomplished rustic-toy builder who often gives classes in rustic-toy building at the Adirondack Museum in Blue Mountain Lake, New York.

Though he's successful, Barry's personality remains disarming. His soft-spoken manner immediately puts people at ease. Barry's charm is somehow translated into his furniture. This and the durable beauty of his work are the reasons for his popularity as a rustic furniture maker.

ABOVE: Set of dining room chairs by Barry Gregson. The molded seats add greatly to the comfort of the chairs.

ABOVE: Birch-bark work by Gregson.

BELOW: Outdoor bench by Gregson.

ABOVE: Yellow birch-bark rockers by Jack Leadley of Speculator, New York. Leadley is widely regarded for the artistry of his work in both furniture and basketry.

Jack Leadley

A LEGEND in the business, Jack Leadley is a folk hero from the past. Few people on the planet today match his strength of character and passion for living. He describes himself as the happiest man in the Adirondacks. Now in his late sixties, Jack has had a life rich in craftsmanship and adventure. He has made snowshoes and baskets for more than thirty years and is widely regarded as the most accomplished pack-basket maker alive today.

As a youth, Jack did what was necessary to stay alive, working on the family farm and later in saw-mills. He spent thirty-three winters trapping beaver in western Canada, where he would walk an average of thirty miles each day on snowshoes to check his trapline. He still runs a sugar-maple operation for maple syrup at his home in Speculator, New York. In his small roadside shop, he also sells his own water-color paintings and other crafts created by both him and his wife, Joan, whom he freely admits is the most important person in his life.

In later years, Jack became enamored with the works of legend-ary Adirondack rustic-builder Lee Fountain, who was prolific in the 1930s. Jack now makes yellow-birch rockers in the Lee Fountain style.

All of Jack's furniture is made completely by hand; there are no power tools or electricity in his workshop. He finds and cuts his own materials and splits and shaves by hand the ash weaving material that he uses for the seats and backs of his chairs and rockers. Each rocker requires between twenty and thirty-five hours for construction, and the waiting list for both his furniture and baskets is quite long. To own a pair of Jack Leadley rockers is consid-ered by many to be an honor, since their comfort, durability, and aes-thetics are highly regarded.

Jack never veered from the furniture-making calling of art in his life. His blue eyes sparkle as he speaks of long winter walks in the woods by himself. His energy is incredibly infectious, and his physical fitness is the cause of great envy in men half his age.

Glenn
Burleigh

GLENN BURLEIGH is a relative newcomer to the rustic furniture business. A professional river guide and forest-firefighter for many years, he developed a profound knowledge and respect for nature. He started making rustic furniture in 1992 between river trips.

Glenn's pieces can best be described as fantasy furniture. They seem to emanate from another dimension. His use of broad lines, oversized materials, and the inherent twists and contortions in the wood add greatly to the element of humor and fantasy in his works. One might expect to see the seven dwarfs or trolls seated at the dining table and chairs that he enjoys building. His works are surprisingly comfortable and structurally sound.

Glenn works out of a small garage in Sisters, Oregon, where his mother is the retired city mayor. He sells his works privately and does little to attract new customers. He is one of many around the country who maintain a very low profile and who builds rustic furniture out of sheer passion for the organic qualities of nature.

LEFT: Glen Burleigh at home in Oregon.

BELOW: Juniper chair by Glenn Burleigh. The texturing and wild organic qualities of juniper trees add to the presence of furniture that they eventually become.

ABOVE: Fantasy dining room set by Glenn Burleigh.

Clifton Monteith

CLIFTON MONTEITH is one of the most highly regarded artists in the country. As a youth he spent much of his free time in his grandfather's wood shop. In time, he received a Master of Fine Arts degree and taught painting, drawing, and sculpture. He spent many years in Manhattan, working in advertising and design.

In 1985, Clifton built himself a twig chair, and a friend talked him into selling it. From that time on, he was in the rustic furniture business full time. Now living in Michigan, he has created over five hundred pieces of rustic furnishings that have been eagerly purchased by collectors of his works. He sells through a few galleries in the Midwest but mostly through private contacts.

Many artists describe themselves as being influenced by various craftsmen as well as different styles of furniture. Clifton's principal and sustaining influence comes from walking through the woods. The many forms and shapes inherent in nature compel him to create in the fashion of nature. He often comments that his extended stay in New York City deprived him of his art and his closeness with nature. His return to natural settings has now rejuvenated his energy and inspirations.

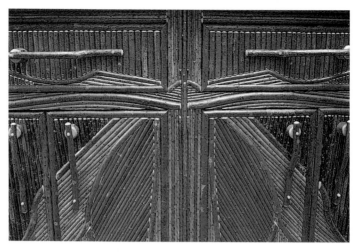

PREVIOUS PAGE: Armchair by Montieth.

ABOVE: Details of Montieth piece.

RIGHT: Hall mirror by Montieth.

ABOVE: Case piece by Clifton Montieth. Clifton is one of very few who have elevated their craftsmanship to the level of the artistic. His pieces often suggest a cubist influence.

Clifton is an extraordinarily bright and articulate individual, and when he is away from his workshop, conversations with him tend to go on for hours, involving a wide variety of esoteric subjects.

Complex, original, and *intricate* are words that describe Clifton's work. The delicate strands of willow applied to the furniture seem to almost flow in a wavelike motion across its surfaces. The mosaic designs inlaid in the furniture follow no traditional pattern but seem to blend naturally with the other elements on the piece. Almost all his pieces are artistically three-dimensional, meaning that they look quite stunning from any angle.

Clifton is certainly one of the most innovative and original designers and builders of rustic furniture of this century. His use of space and motion put him significantly ahead of his time, and one might think of Picasso and the cubist movement when examining certain areas of his furniture.

Clifton is widely recognized internationally, and several major collections of contemporary art include his works.

LEFT: Built-in bed table by Montieth. An original Dirk Van Erp lamp provides light for reading on the long Maine winter nights.

Lionel Maurier

Lionel's most accomplished works, however, are his kitchens. An expert cabinetmaker, Lionel covers his cupboards with detailed mosaic and bark coverings in the classical Adirondack style. He often spends weeks designing and constructing one kitchen.

Lionel is a pleasure to be around, although he is an arch conservative who constantly offers opinions on the economy and world affairs. Nonetheless, his lightheartedness and bantering personality puts people at ease.

An avid fisherman and hunter, Lionel takes great pleasure in hiking through the woods, finding appropriate materials for his projects. He cuts material for many of his projects during the cold winter months when the bark will adhere to the wood. He also cuts numerous ash trees during this time that will become the legs for his tables. Material collected by Lionel is stored for many months to ensure adequate drying. During the summer, when the sap is not running and the black flies are biting, Lionel strips birch trees of their bark for use on case pieces such as cupboards and bookcases.

LIONEL MAURIER comes to the rustic-furniture business by way of the log-home industry. He has personally built more than twenty-five log homes. He started building rustic furniture at the request of a client in 1988. Today, Lionel is recognized for his superb craftsmanship and attention to detail.

Lionel works in a variety of different styles. It is not uncommon to visit his workshop and find massive settees intricately constructed of apple-tree roots and branches, finely crafted Adirondack cupboards covered with birch bark, or huge beds made of birch and ash logs. He is also known to build wonderful desks and other pieces covered with intricate mosaic patterns such as mountains and forests.

ABOVE: Lionel Maurier on one of his apple-branch settees.

PREVIOUS PAGE: Mosaic drop-front desk by Maurier. Lionel often creates rustic scenes in his furniture such as the one pictured.

RIGHT: High-tech kitchen created by Maurier. The cupboards are lined with birch bark and trimmed with mosaic twig work.

ABOVE: Birch-bark cupboard and bunk beds fit comfortably into this small Adirondack guest room.

Lionel, like so many other successful builders, usually starts work before the sun is up and often works late at night, meticulously, on a piece of his artwork. Like other builders, he finds that the use of modern tools greatly enhances the quality of his furniture. His workshop, deep in the northern New Hampshire woods, is complete with high-tech tools and hundreds of logs and branches waiting to be turned into functional furniture.

Sampson Bog

BARNEY AND SUSAN BELLINGER of Mayfield, New York, operate a small gallery called Sampson Bog, named after a secluded trout-fishing lake in the Adirondacks. From their gallery Barney and Susan, along with their daughter, Erin, produce some of the finest and most original rustic furniture available today.

Barney has worked with wood since the early seventies and began working in the rustic mode in 1989. He is primarily responsible for the intricate paintings that adorn each piece produced in his studio. His paintings are actual scenes that come from the Adirondacks, or clients can bring in photographs from their favorite areas and have them rendered into paintings on Barney's furniture. His wife, Susan, and protege, Peter Winter, are responsible for much of the twig-and-bark work on the pieces. His four-year-old daughter, Erin, also works in the family business, applying pine cones and acorns and collecting twigs that eventually become part of the furniture.

Sampson Bog pieces are most closely related to the Adirondack style. Twigs are carefully fused in delicate mosaic patterns, and antlers are often applied to add grace and balance. Pine cones, acorns, and other natural materials are often included to further embellish the pieces. The colors of the varying pieces produced are remarkably accurate renditions of the rich hues one would see in the woods. The pieces are by no means "new looking," but rather they have been produced to present a "mellow, aged look." More than any other builder in the country, their pieces seem to blend with their environment. Items produced by the gallery include desks, shelving units, tables of varying sizes, and other items requested by clients.

LEFT: Delicate root-based stand from the New York studio of Sampson Bog.

Certainly the most striking attributes of Sampsom Bog pieces are their sophistication, delicacy, and form. Each piece is truly one-of-a-kind, and great consideration is given to the artistic quality of each endeavor. Respect for each piece is a phrase that is frequently heard around the gallery.

Articles about Sampson Bog have appeared in *Country Living Magazine*, *Adirondack Life*, and other publications. Many major collections around the country include a piece from the Sampson Bog workshop, and knowledgeable, nationally known decorators frequently commission them to produce pieces for high-end decorating projects.

LEFT: Fly-fishing desk by Sampson Bog.

Elkhorn Designs

RICHARD KEENE began his working career as an electric lineman and in 1985 began building ornate chandeliers, tables, chairs, and decorative accessories out of elk antlers. Today, he operates a gallery in Jackson Hole, Wyoming, appropriately called Elkhorn Design.

Richard is a man of few words. His furniture, however, is stunning. He employs nine individuals, including his wife and sister-in-law. And though he operates a large shop, his pieces are individually designed and handcrafted.

Purchasing elk antlers by the pound for his many projects, Richard also uses fallow deer antlers from Europe, moose, and caribou antlers. All his chandeliers are internally wired, and his was the first company to be approved by the Underwriters Laboratory. The antlers for his furniture are completely bolted together, and great care is taken to produce structurally sound pieces.

Of utmost concern to Richard is the comfort of the many chairs and settees produced by his firm. These pieces are eventually upholstered in leather and, in the decorative sense, fit into a variety of living situations.

Not only does Richard sell from his shop, he also exhibits his strikingly original work at a number of other galleries throughout the West and Rocky Mountain states.

ABOVE: Elk-antler bench and related accessories by Elkhorn Designs.

NEXT PAGE: Antler artistry by Richard Keene of Elkhorn Designs.

Arcadia Wood Works

RUSTIC-BUILDER Lester Santos is the son of a carpenter, and as a youth, he spent many years working with his father in the building business. In 1970, Lester began building harpsichords. From there he opened a cabinet shop and later began building guitars until 1976. At that time, he moved to Cody, Wyoming, where he honed his carpentry skills by rebuilding houses.

In 1990, he went to work as a designer and builder for Sweet Water Ranch, a firm specializing in western rustic furniture. By 1994, however, he struck out on his own and purchased a section of an old hotel formerly owned by Thomas Molesworth. He had the building moved to his property and opened Arcadia Wood Works.

The company specializes in one-of-a-kind rustic pieces and takes commissions for a wide variety of furnishings, including chairs, tables, and related objects in the rustic style.

Lester is a low-key, unassuming man of great talent. He seeks to incorporate Adirondack and western designs into his furniture and prefers to manipulate, as little as possible, woods used in his projects. Most of his pieces are constructed out of juniper, although he occasionally uses other materials as well. He spends hours collecting his own materials and often rejects dead trees for his own use if they look beautiful where they are.

Once Lester acquires materials from the forest near his home in Cody, he places the wood in an old school bus that has had the seats removed. "The bus" he says, "is an ideal kiln and dries the wood perfectly."

The carvings on Lester's pieces, all done by hand, are masterful. He prefers to carve scenes that come directly from where the tree was originally found, and mountains and trees are often the subjects of his inscriptions. As a rule Lester replaces the dead trees he uses with new seedlings and is probably the only builder who makes a cash contribution to the forest service from each piece of furniture he sells.

Lester's items are sold in galleries throughout the Rocky Mountains and from his own gallery in Cody. His work is highly sought after and has been featured in magazines such as *Southwest Art* and others.

ABOVE: Burled cedar armchair by Lester Santos of Arcadia Woodworks. Lester creates unique pieces that evoke the wilderness spirit of the American West.

Nick
Nickerson

FOR THE FIRST twenty-five years of his life, Nick Nickerson worked in the advertising business as a photographer and eventually as an art director in New York City. Then, in 1990, he decided to experiment with rustic furniture. Today, his works are in a class by themselves. In his workshop in the Adirondacks, he creates the most stunning mirrors available today.

Nick works with a variety of different woods including birch, locust, maple, oak, cedar, and hickory. He also travels many miles from his home to harvest bittersweet bark in Pennsylvania for different projects.

Nick is the first to admit that he is neither a skilled carpenter nor a cabinetmaker. Rather, he approaches his work as sculpture or collage and often refers to his projects as puzzles. Some of his

mirror frames contain as many as one hundred tiny pieces of bark that were meticulously chosen and placed together to work in conjunction with the frame as a whole. It is time-consuming work. He works by himself, and on the average, he spends between twenty and thirty hours on each mirror. Large mirrors require many more hours. He approaches his efforts as art and not a craft. While working, he often saves different-colored sawdust that can later be used to fill in needed spaces.

Nick's mirrors have an organic quality to them, and they literally seem to ripple like a wave across water. They appear to come to life as the movement contained within them speaks to the viewer. It is nearly impossible to see any breaks or joints on the surface of his works. It appears that they are one large

piece of bark, when in reality, they are many pieces combined together.

Like many other builders, Nick sells his work through different galleries. He also receives commissions from many admirers of his work around the country, and he exhibits at the Rustic Furniture Builders Show at the Adirondack Museum each fall.

ABOVE: Organic frames by Nick Nickerson of the Adirondacks.

LEFT: Birch-bark frame by Nick Nickerson. Nick's frames almost seem to come alive as they contain striking fluidity and movement within their boundaries.

David Robinson

DAVID ROBINSON was intro-
duced to the art world when he
worked ten years for a sculptor in
San Francisco. Then, in 1981, he
was hired by New York City to
restore the wonderful rustic gazebos, wooden bridges, pergolas, and
settees that reside in Central Park.
Initially, he spent considerable time
researching the various designs that
the Victorian builders used in their
outdoor structures.

Eventually, David restored many
of the existing structures based on
early designs and also built two new
large gazebos and many settees,
bridges, and rustic fences that add
rugged ambiance to Central Park.

Surprisingly, David does not
consider himself an artist. He
modestly (and correctly) mentions
that anyone can build simple rustic
furniture. The art, he says, is finding the right materials and putting
them together in such a way as to
make them artistic.

David is a matter-of-fact person
who does not dwell on long conversations involving philosophical or
artistic principles. He forgoes the
art world, he says, to make a living.
Modest as he is, his gazebos, fences,
gates, and bridges are striking
additions to the many parks and
yards fortunate to be home to his
work. Walking among his work in
Central Park, one gets the distinct
feeling of being in the wilds. His
careful designs and meticulous

ABOVE: This stunning bedroom suite by David Robinson is at the Lake Placid Lodge in the
Adirondacks.

construction techniques ensure that
his work will be enjoyed by viewers
for many years to come.

More than half of the items that
come from David's shop, such as
gazebos and settees, are made for
the outdoors. The remainder of his
work is rustic tables, chairs, and
other furniture that is traditionally
used indoors.

Like many advanced builders,
David's chairs are surprisingly
comfortable and sturdy. His outdoor
settees appear as though they have
grown up from the ground, and his
beds are uniquely organic and well
constructed. Each piece built by
David is uniquely different from all
of his other pieces. No one, he says,
wants the exact same piece that his
neighbor has.

David primarily uses cedar for
his outdoor furniture because of its
resistance to insects and decompo-
sition. Other woods used by him are
black locust, mulberry, and Osage

orange. He mentions that he uses
either a free-form, organic look that
includes twisted and gnarled
branches and roots or some of his
clients prefer a more geometrical
look with discernable patterns
throughout. He says that he has no
preference but enjoys working with
both styles.

David's work is widely recognized, and articles about him and
his work have appeared in over
fifteen different national publications. He sells primarily from his
shop in Pennington, New Jersey,
and works with architects and
decorators around the country.

Ken Heitz

KEN HEITZ is one of the originals in the rustic-furniture business. Prior to a career in rustic furniture, he worked for IBM for several years and moved to the Adirondacks, where he took a job in a sawmill. Eventually, the mill burned down, and he was out of work. Necessity being the mother of invention, he one day realized he needed several pieces of new furniture and something to do until a job came around, so in 1974 he started building rustic furniture.

For the first five years, the majority of Ken's business was in New York City, and he made monthly trips to the city with a load of rustic furniture on the back of his pickup truck. In time, his business expanded and he began taking orders from a wide variety of designers, decorators, and architects.

Today, articles about Ken have appeared in dozens of national publications. Ken's furniture not only resides in numerous homes across America, but restaurants, lodges, hotels, and museums have pieces of his furniture as well. Customers can order pieces pictured in his catalogues, or he builds things from the drawings and wishes of his clients.

Ken is a completely self-taught craftsman. At the heart of his efforts is the underlying principle that he wanted his furniture to be useful and functional. He wanted it to be passed down through generations.

He works with a variety of hardwoods, including ironwood, white ash, and white and yellow birch. The wood he uses is completely kiln-dried and chosen for its sturdiness and aesthetic qualities.

LEFT: Ken uses a wide variety of woods in his projects and has worked in the traditional style for many years.

Throughout the years, Ken has created just about every piece of furniture imaginable including massive beds, settees and chairs, huge tables, clocks, lamps, and other items. He works in the classic Adirondack style. His applied birch-bark pieces and intricate mosaic pieces are well constructed and designed. Pieces that he made many years ago have withstood the test of time and abuse.

Much of Ken's furniture is found in public places such as lodges and restaurants, and it is subject to constant use. Throughout the years, his pieces have mellowed to rich colors and are comfortable as well as sturdy.

Ken works by himself at his shop in Indian Lake, New York, in the heart of the Adirondacks. His workshop, like the shop of almost all other builders, is a visual feast of woods, tools, partially made furniture, and completed projects. Outside his shop are two twenty-five-foot-tall chairs that certainly get the attention of passersby.

ABOVE: Bunk beds and bedroom furniture by Ken Heitz.

RIGHT: Bureau by Ken Heitz.

Resource List for Rustic Furniture Makers

The following makers are listed alphabetically, not by furniture style.
However, the following key was devised to aid the reader:

Adirondack—Ad   Antler—Ant

Willow—Wl   Hickory—H

Free Form—FF   Gazebos—G

Western—W   Bent Twig—BT

Greg Adams—Wl, BT
P.O. Box 745
Lapel, IN 46051
(317) 534-3009

Added Oomph!—BT
P.O. Box 6135
High Point, NC 27262
(910) 886-4410

Paul "Kid" Allen—Ant
401 E. Douglas Road
Ft. Collins, CO 80524
(970) 482-7102

American Twig—FF
70 N. Main Street
Homer, NY 13077

The Amish Country Collection—BT
P.O. Box 5085
New Castle, PA 16105
(412) 458-4811

Andrea and Phillip—Ad
P.O. Box 131
Palenville, NY 12463

Appalachian Rustic Furniture
1085 N. Main
Blowing Rock, NC 28605
(704) 295-9554

Arizona Ranch—W
1300A East 8th Street
Tempe, AZ 85281
(602) 921-1101

Barney, Susan, and Erin
Bellinger—Ad
Sampson Bog Studio
171 Paradise Point
Mayfield, NY 12117
(518) 661-6563

Glen Bauer—Ad
Box 77, Route 3
Vermontville, NY 12989
(518) 891-5104

The Bear's Hand
R.D. 1, Box 111C
Schroon Lake, NY 12870

Beaver Chew
Box 23
Elkins, NH 03233
(603) 526-2319

Andy Brown
Hearthwoods Rustic Furnishings
110 N. Whittaker
New Buffalo, MI 49117
(616) 469-5551

Burl Country—FF
Forrest and Pat Willis
1889 Eel River Drive
Fortuna, CA 95540
(707) 725-3982

Glen Burleigh
Box 106
Powell Butte, OR 97753
(514) 548-6913

Jerry Cihak—FF
Just Driftin'
13636 Southwestern
Blue Island, IL 60406
(708) 489-5238

Tim and Gloria Clark—Wl
The Willow Shop
P.O. Box 412
Lawton, MI 49065
(616) 624-7268

Tom Clark—W
TEC Woodsmithing
8127 W. 71st Place
Arvada, CO 80004
(303) 422-9021

Phil Clausen
Rt. 1, Box 3397
Coquille, OR 97423
(503) 396-4806

Diane Cole—W
Rustic Furniture
10 Cloninger Lane
Bozeman, MT 59715
(406) 586-3746

Diane and Indy Corson—W
Lupine Log Arts
13750 Kelly Canyon
Bozeman, MT 59715
(406) 587-0672

Jimmy and Lynda Covert—W
Covert Workshops
Cody, WY 82414

Margaret Craven
14 Twelfth Avenue
Longmont, CO 80501
(303) 772-1951

Kimberly K. Crofts—W
Salmon River Naturals
P.O. Box 1433
Hailey, ID 83333
(208) 788-3252

Crystal Farms—Ant
Antler Chandeliers and Furniture
18 Antelope Road
Redstone, CO 81623
(970) 963-2350

Gary Dannels—BT
Beacon Woodcraft
P. O. Box 11
Beacon, IA 52534
(515) 673-6210

Jay Dawson—Ad
R.D. 1, Box 257
Lake Clear, NY 12945
(518) 891-5075

Devonshire—BT
P.O. Box 760
Middleburg, VA 22117
(703) 687-5990

Lillian Dodson—Ad
133 Crooked Hill Road
Huntington, NY 11743
(516) 427-2750

ABOVE: The storage yard of Brent McGregor. The juniper trees will eventually become beds and floor lamps.

PREVIOUS PAGE: Classic Adirondack sideboard by George Jacques of Keene Valley, New York.

ABOVE: Burled lodge-pole pines that will eventually become rustic furniture are dried for months prior to use.

Barry Gregson—Ad
Adirondack Rustics Gallery
Charlie Hill Road
Box 88
Schroon Lake, NY 12870
(518) 532-9384

Dave Hall—Ad
Adirondack Furniture and Art
P.O. Box 321
Bloomingdale, NY 12913
(518) 523-2697

Frank Hamm—Ad
Out of the Woods
341 Beacon Street #3E
Boston, MA 02116
(617) 899-5752 or
(617) 236-1086

Karl Hanck—Ad
Starbuck Road
P.O. Box 89
Fort Ann, NY 12827

Bobby Hansson—Ad
2068 Tome Highway
Port Deposit, MD 21904
(410) 658-3959

Bud Hanzlick—Ad
Bekan Rustic Furniture
P.O. Box 323
Belleville, KS 66935
(913) 527-2427

Jerry Hauk—W, FF
Western Plains Design Studio
1522.5 Broadway
Scottsbluff, NE 69361
(308) 635-6862

Ken Heitz—Ad
Backwoods Furnishings
Box 161, Rt. 28
Indian Lake, NY 12412
(518) 251-3327

Hellers Fabulous Furniture—FF
Rt. 28
Boiceville, NY 12412
(914) 657-6317

ABOVE: The backyards of almost all rustic builders are storage areas for materials.

Andrew Himmen—Ad
75 Pequot Rd.
Southhampton, MA 01073
(413) 538-8745

The Homestead—Ad
10249 Oswego Fishtrap Lake Road
Boulder Junction, WI 54512
(715) 385 2428

Jim Howard—Ad
P.O. Box 413
Long Lake, NY 12847
(518) 624-3813

Liz Hunt—BT
Box 218176
Columbus, OH 43221
(614) 459-1551

Richard and Lisa Ianni—BT
A-Ya Art
P.O. Box 23
Street Johnsville, NY 13452
(518) 568-5015

George Jacques—Ad
Box 545, Main Street
Keene Valley, NY 12943
(518) 576-2214

Stuart Johnstone—Ad
Wicopi Studios
P.O. Box 87
Chestertown, NY 12817
(518) 494-2171

Richard Keene
Elkhorn Designs
P.O. Box 7663
Jackson Hole, WY 83001
(307) 733-4655

ABOVE: Sideboard by master western builders Jimmy and Lynda Covert of Cody, Wyoming.

ABOVE: Stumps, twigs, roots, branches, and other natural material—the rustic furniture maker's dream.

La Lune Collection—BT
930 E. Burleigh
Milwaukee, WI 53212
(414) 263-5300

Tom Latshaw—BT
Rustic Furniture
RD 2, Box 12
New Paris, PA 15554
(814) 839-2691

Laughing Willows—Wl
Partington Ridge
Big Sur, CA 93920
(408) 667-2133

Jack Leadley—Ad
P.O. Box 142
Speculator, NY 12164
(518) 548-7093

Jake Lemon—FF, W
Woodworker
P.O. Box 2404
Sun Valley, ID 83353
(208) 788-3004

Jackson Levi-Smith—Ad
RD 1, Box 543
Osborne Hill
Herkimer, NY 13350
(315) 866-6789

Lodgepole Manufacturing—W
Star Rt. 15
Jackson, WY 83001
(307) 733-3199

Michael Long—W
Wyoming Polecrafter
HCR 61 Box 303
Thayne, WY 83127
(307) 883-2946

James McGee—Wl
P.O. Box 645
Spring City, TN 37381

Brent McGregor—FF
Rocky Mountain Timber Products
P.O. Box 1477
Sisters, OR 97759
(505) 549-1322

Daniel Mack—Ad
Rustic Furnishings
14 Welling Avenue
Warwick, NY
(212) 691-1143

Matt Madsen/Tim Duncan—FF
Burl Art West
P.O. Box 187
Orick, CA 95555
(707) 488-3795

Master Thatchers—G
#1 Creek Road
Christiana, PA 17509
(610) 593-2468

Masterworks—Wl
P.O. Box M
Marietta, GA 30061
(404) 423-9000

Tom Matz—W
Rustic Log Furniture
6040 Lake Patricia Dr.
East Jordan, MI 49727
(616) 536-7288

Lionel Maurier—Ad
Rustic Renditions
26 Tucker Mountain Rd.
Meredith, NH 03253
(603) 279-4320

Rob Mazza—W
Willow Run Woodworking
2330 Amsterdam Road
Belgrade, MT 59714
(406) 388-6848

Glenn A. Monson—Ad
Blue Mountain Woods
1025 N. 100 W.
Orem, UT 84057
(801) 224-1347

Clifton Montieth—Wl
Twiggery
P.O. Box 9
Lake Ann, MI 49650
(616) 275-6560

Nature's Design—Wl
Dan Quinn
103 Wilson Creek Road
Cullowhee, NC 28723
(704) 293-7155

Nelson Handcrafters—Wl
1013 Palo Alto Road
Sequim, WA 98382
(206) 681-0729

Nick Nickerson—Ad
Forest Furniture
P.O. Box 618
Copake, NY 12516
(518) 329-1664

BELOW: Pair of rustic settees by Clifton Montieth.

BELOW: Antler furniture by Crystal Farms of Colorado.

Old Hickory—H
403 S. Noble Street
Shelbyville, IN 46176
(800) 232-2275

Susan Parish—W
2898 Glascock
Oakland, CA 94601
(510) 261-0353

Phillip and Kathy Payne—Wl
Rt. 3, Box 1020
Broadhead, KY 40409
(606) 758-8587

John and Gary Phillips—W
The Drawknife
99 West Highway 33
Tetonia, ID 83452
1-800-320-0527

Tom Phillips—Ad
Star Rt. 2
Tupper Lake, NY 12986
(518) 359-9648

William Pryor—Ad
Hawk Feather
R.D. 1, Box 117 A-1
Smyrna, NY 13464
(607) 627-6784

Pure and Simple—Wl
117 W. Hempstead
P.O. Box 535
Nashville, AR 71852

E. N. Raber—Wl
Pope Rd.
Randolph, NY 14772

Ragged Mountain Antler
Chandeliers—Ant
106 Meadow Lane
Marble, CO 81623
(800) 963-0708

David Robinson—Ad, G
Natural Edge
515 Tuxford Ct.
Trenton, NJ 08638
(609) 737-8996

Romancing the Woods—G
33 Raycliffe Drive
Woodstock, NY 12498
(914) 246-6976

Abby Ruoff—Ad
Wood-Lot Farms
Star Rt. 1
Shady, NY 12409
(914) 679-8084

Rustic Ranch Furnishings—W
Rt. 4, Box 363C
Terrell, TX 75160
(214) 524-8894

Ronald Sanborn—Ad
Hulls Falls Rd.
Keene, NY 12942
(813) 625-7207

Lester Santos—W
Arcadia Woodworks
2208 Public Street
Cody, WY 82414
(307) 587-6543

Dick Schindeldecker—W, FF
Box 192
Ione, WA 99139
(509) 442-3249

Crispin Shakeshaft—Ad
R.R. 1, Box 25
Crown Point, NY 12928
(518) 597-3304

Ron and Jean Shanor—W,FF
Wildwood Furniture
P.O. Box 1631
Cody, WY 82414
(307) 587-9558

John and Shirl Stacy—Ad
Lean 2 Studio
P.O. Box 222
Adirondack, NY 12808
(518) 494-5185

Dennis Smith—Ad
R.F.D. 3
Malone, NY 12953
(518) 483-8108

ABOVE: Armchair by Hellers Fabulous Furniture of New York.

Peter Sparks—Ad
Waterfront Hoop Back
P.O. Box 4161
Burlington, VT 05406

Timothy Hayes Rustic Furniture—
    Ad
R.R. 1, Box 168
Brattleboro, VT 05301
(802) 254-8448

Dwayne R. Thompson—Ad
Timpson Creek Mill Works
Rt. 2, Box 2117 Hwy. 76
Clayton, GA 30525
(706) 782-5164

Tiger Mountain Woodworks—H, Ad,
    Wl
Paul Moody and Barry Jones
P.O. Box 1088
Hwy. 106
Highlands, NC 28741
(704) 526-5577

Hutch Travers—Ad
Rt. 1, Box 230
Wake Forrest, NC 27587
(919) 582-0458

David Vana—Ad
276 Averyville Rd.
Lake Placid, NY 12946
(518) 523-1899

Susan Van Pelt—W
Box 335
Gallatin-Gateway, MT 59730
(406) 763-4887

Micki Voisard—Ad
999 Conn Valley Rd.
St. Helena, CA 94574
(707) 963-8364

Jack Waller—Ad
P.O. Box 1
Phillipsburg, MT 59858
406 859-3564

Judd Weisberg
Rt. 42
Lexington, NY 12452
(518) 989-6583

Peggy Yoder—Wl
Hickory Rockers of Berlin
Box 235
Berlin, OH 44610
(216) 893-2680

ABOVE: The rustic antler work of Paul Allen of Fort Collins, Colorado.

Galleries

ABC Carpet
888 Broadway
New York, NY 10003
(212) 473-3000

Adirondack Store and Gallery
109 Saranac Avenue
Lake Placid, NY 12946
(518) 523-2646

Adirondack Trading Post
91 Main Street
Lake Placid, NY 12946
(518) 891-6278

Black Mountain Antique Mall
100 Sutton Avenue
Black Mountain, NC 28711
(704) 669-6218

Davis/Torres Antiques
14 West Main
Bozeman, MT 59715
(406) 587-1587

Garden Living
206 Sutton
Black Mountain, NC 28711

Jordan Gallery
1349 Sheridan Avenue
Cody, WY 82414
(307) 587-6689

Lake Placid Antique Center
103 Main Street
Lake Placid, NY 12946
(518) 523-3913

Newel Art Gallery
425 East 53rd
New York, NY 10012
(212) 758-1970

Ralph Kylloe Gallery
Rt. 9N
Lake Luzerne Road
Lake George, NY 03053
(518) 696-5182

Sticks and Stones
3680 Galleria
Edina, MN 55435
(612) 926-5337

Summer House in Highlands
Third at Spring Street
Highlands, NC 28741
(704) 526-9414

Whispering Pines
510 Main Street
Piermont, NY 10968
(914) 359-6302

ABOVE: Very rare lamp with original mica shade from the Adirondacks.

NEXT PAGE: Chair and lamp by Doug Pickering of Cody, Wyoming.

York Antique
Route 1, Box 303
York, ME 03909
(207) 363-5002